Mel Bay's MORE FUN
VIOLIN

Big Note — Easy Solos   by Bill Bay

More fun with the Violin is a collection of well-known, favorite melodies arranged in solo form for the beginning student. All the music contained in this book was designed to provide the beginning student with a wealth of musical fun and satisfaction. We hope this text will give the student hours of musical enjoyment.

TABLE OF CONTENTS

THE VIOLIN

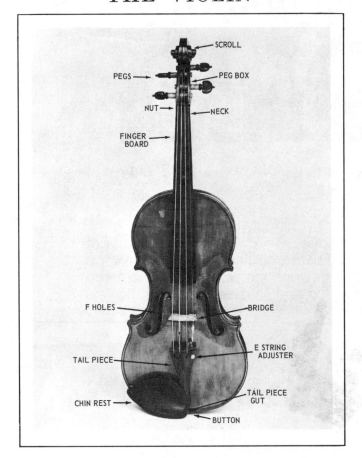

- SCROLL
- PEGS
- PEG BOX
- NUT
- NECK
- FINGER BOARD
- F HOLES
- BRIDGE
- E STRING ADJUSTER
- TAIL PIECE
- TAIL PIECE GUT
- CHIN REST
- BUTTON

THE BOW

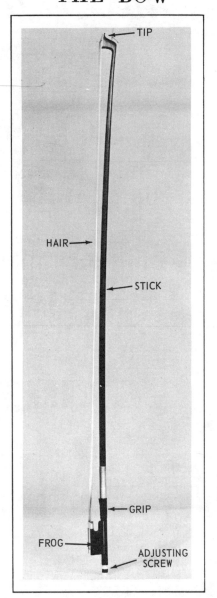

- TIP
- HAIR
- STICK
- GRIP
- FROG
- ADJUSTING SCREW

TUNING THE VIOLIN

First String . . . . E
Second String . . . . A
Third String . . . . D
Fourth String . . . . G

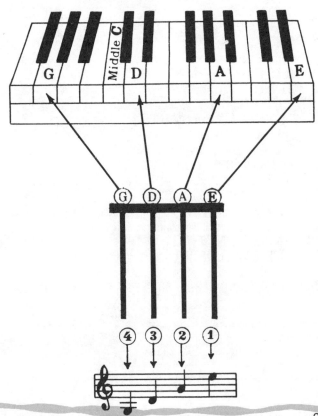

PITCH PIPES

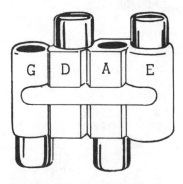

A Pitch Pipe for the Violin may be purchased from any music store. Each pipe will have the correct pitch for each Violin string. A Pitch Pipe is a valuable aid.

Wade in the Water

Medium Swing Tempo

Spiritual

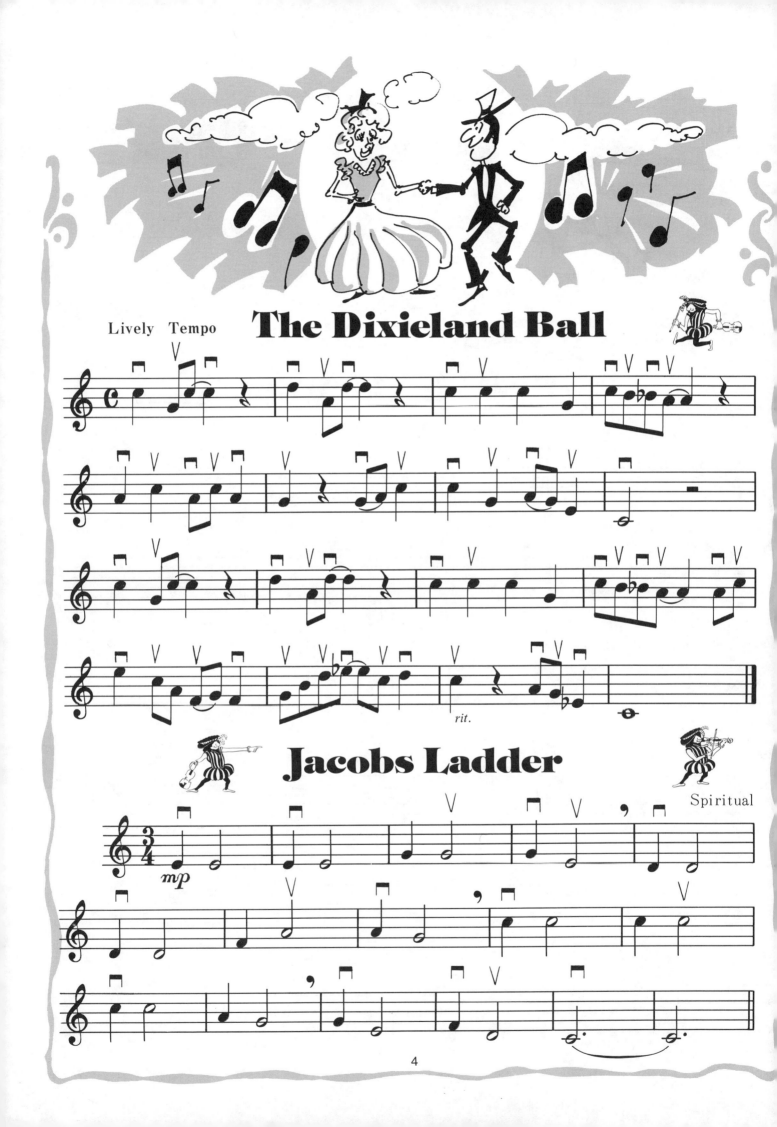

The Dixieland Ball

Lively Tempo

Jacobs Ladder

Spiritual

4

How Firm A Foundation

Early American Hymn

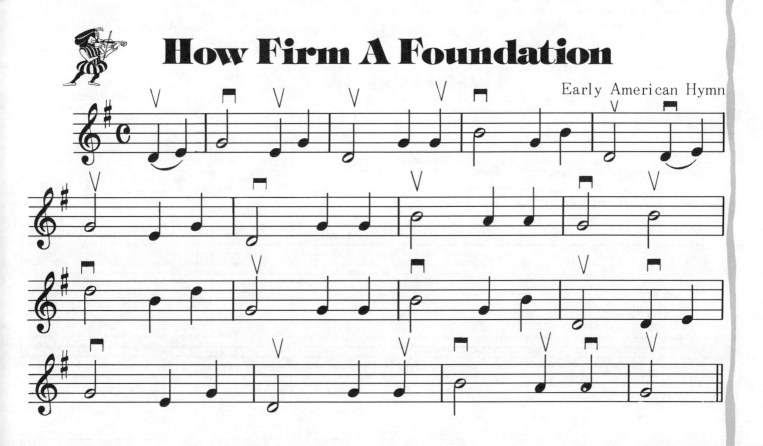

My Bonnie Dearie

Scottish Folk Song

Slowly

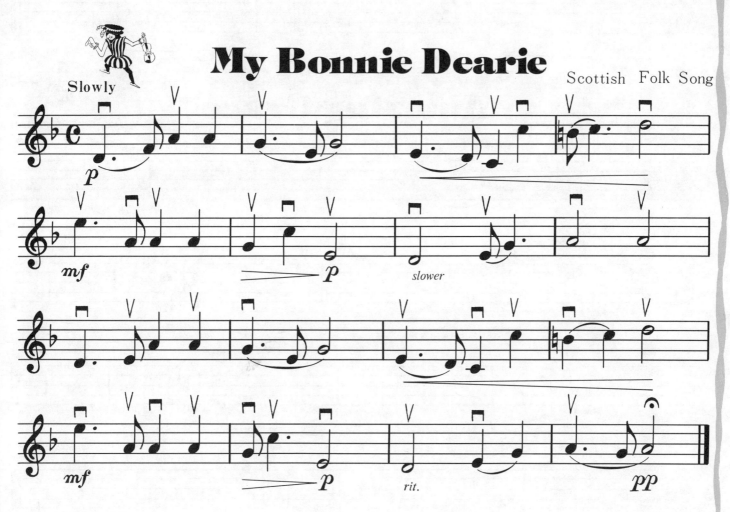

Wondrous Love

Peacefully

Early American Hymn

Amazing Grace

Flowing Tempo

Early American Hymn

6

The Gal I Left Behind Me

Song of the West

Brisk Tempo

O My Darling Clementine

Moderately

mf

Simple Gifts

Shaker Song

America

Ol' Dan Tucker

Fast Tempo

Folk Song

mf

Haul Away Joe

Moderately

Sea Song

The Marines' Hymn

Boldly

The Caissons

Moderat

U.S. Army Song

mf

10

One More Day

Slowly

Sea Chantey

Shady Grove

Old Southern Banjo Tune

Variation

11

Walls of Jericho

Swing Tempo

Spiritual

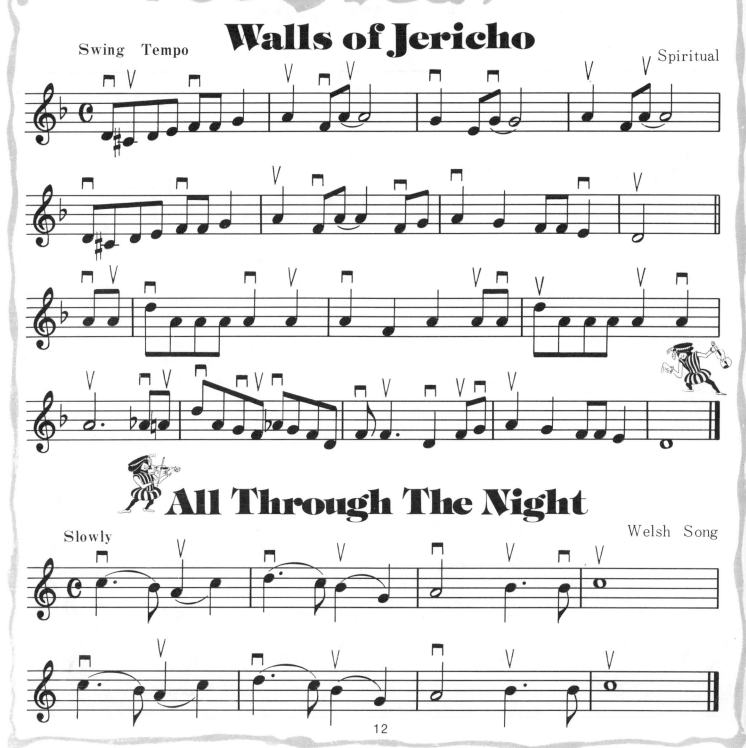

All Through The Night

Slowly

Welsh Song

Blow Ye Winds

Song of the Seas

America, The Beautiful

Katherine Bates

Samuel A. Ward

13

Peacherine Rag

Medium Swing Tempo

Scott Joplin

Sailor's Hornpipe

Medium Tempo

Fiddle Tune

Come And Go With Me

Lively Tempo

Spiritual

The Midnight Special

Swing Tempo

Folk Song

I Know Where I'm Goin'

Slowly

Scottish Hymn

Praise To The Lord

Boldly

Favorite Hymn

16

At A Georgia Camp Meeting

Lively Tempo

Old Banjo Song

Henry Martin

Bright Tempo

Sea Ballad

Little Brown Jug

Swing Tempo

Folk Song

Sunny's Blues

Slowly

Blues Song

Buffalo Gals

Bright Tempo

Western Song

Old Joe Clark

Lively Tempo

Old Banjo Tune

Sailing, Sailing

Cielito Lindo

Flowing Tempo

Mexican Song

Chorus

The Easy Winners

Appalachain Melody

Bright Tempo (In one)

Folk Song

Captain Kidd

Lively Tempo

Sea Song

La Cucaracha

Mexican Dance

23

Chester

Lively Tempo

Song of the Revolutionary War

Gary Owen

Lively Tempo

Bagpipe Song

24

Soldiers Joy

Lively Tempo

Old Fiddle Tune

Go Tell It On The Mountain

Slowly

Spiritual

All My Trials

Medium Tempo

Spiritual

O Come, O Come, Emmanuel

12th Century

Coventry Carol

Slowly

Old English

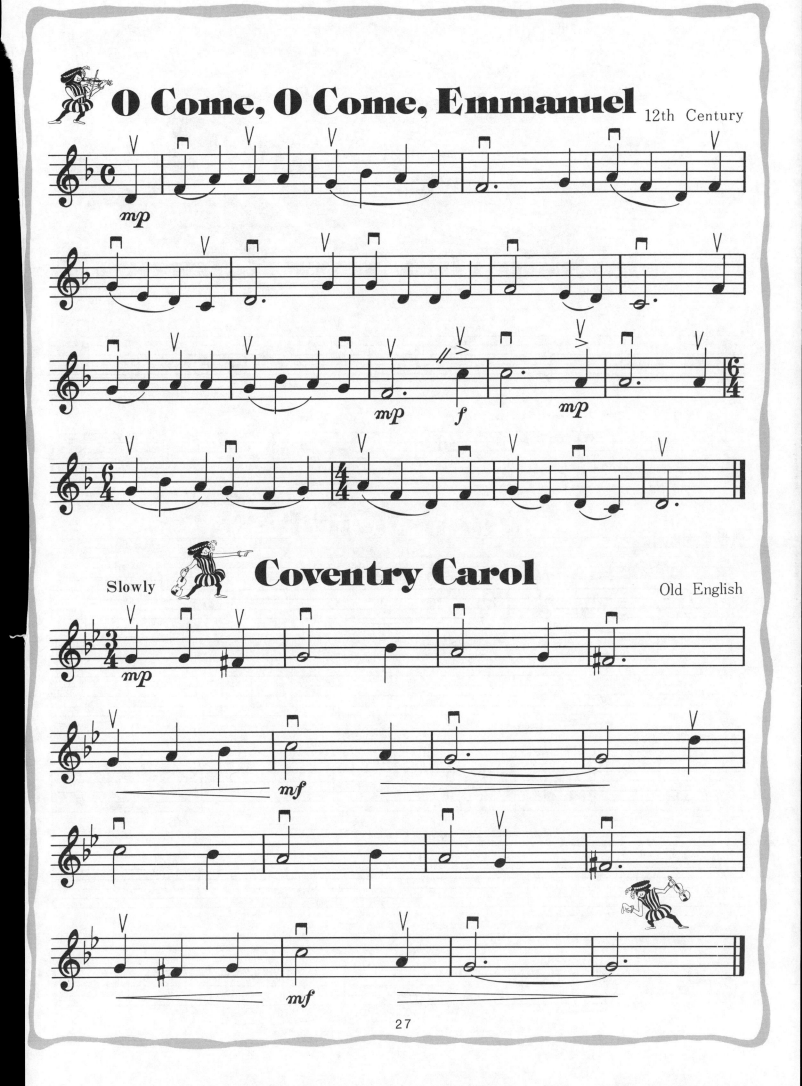

The Ship That Never Returned

Lively Tempo

Sea song

Minor Melody

Slowly

mp *mf*

mp

mf *mp*

Year Of Jubilo

Fast Tempo

Henry Clay Work

Green Grow The Lilacs

Moderately

Folk Song

29

Swanee River

Slowly

Stephen Foster

My Old Kentucky Home

Slowly

Stephen Foster

Chorus

30

Tenting Tonight

Slowly

Civil War Song

rit.

Angels We Have Heard On High

Moderately

French Carol

Ragtime Dance

Medium RAG Tempo

Scott Joplin

Cumberland Gap

Fast Tempo

Banjo Tune